PIE

Nicola Cantan

NICOLA CANTAN is a piano teacher, author, blogger and creator of imaginative and engaging teaching resources from Dublin, Ireland. She loves getting piano students learning through laughter and exploring the diverse world of music making through improvisation, composition and games.

Nicola's membership site, *Vibrant Music Teaching*, is helping teachers all over the world to include more games and off-bench activities in their lessons, so that their students giggle their way through music theory and make faster progress.

Nicola also runs a popular blog, *Colourful Keys*, where she shares creative ideas and teaching strategies, and hosts regular training events for piano teachers.

practice PIE

Nicola Cantan

Colourful Keys Books

Published in the Republic of Ireland

First Printing, 2021

ISBN 978-1-913000-15-8

Colourful Keys
78 Durrow Road
Dublin, D12 V3A3

www.vibrantmusicteaching.com

To all the wonderful parents in my own piano studio, past and present.

Contents

Introduction

Accept Your Apron

Why Bake a Practice Pie?

So you've picked up this book (or someone put it in your hand) and cracked the spine. Congratulations! You're already taking a step that many parents never will. You're thinking about how to best support your child in their musical journey.

However, I doubt you're fully on board yet. You value music, sure. You know how many benefits it has for your child's development and emotional wellbeing, and how enriching it could be in their life.

But do you really have to bake a metaphorical practice pie? That sounds like a whole lot of effort and time you don't really have. Isn't there a store-bought option or, better yet, a home delivery service for practice pie?

Unfortunately not. You might luck out and have one of those kids who manages to muddle through and find their own motivation and methods of practising.

But I can tell you from experience that those kiddos are less than 1% of the population. And those that don't naturally go to their instrument to practise of their own volition or practise in constructive ways week after week and year after year are no less "talented" or "musical". They just need a little help.

IF YOUR CHILD CAN'T BAKE ALONE…

I chose the pie analogy for this book for many reasons. I like how it encourages us to see things in layers and that the process is iterative – you can always return to the mixing bowl and start a new pie. It's also fun and silly, and I hope that element brings some playfulness into the practice process, since it can be a point of tension in many families.

But another reason I want you to picture the perfect practice pie is so that you understand how complex this is for your child. If someone gave you a recipe, you have enough adulting skills to follow it and bake the pie. Even if you have a baking aversion, I don't think we need to fear that you'll set fire to the house or cause yourself irreparable harm.

Depending on the age of your child, however, you most likely wouldn't let them bake a pie alone. If they're six, you might get them involved with the stirring and have them help you pour the filling into the crust. If they're nine, maybe they can chop the apples with your supervision and set the timer according to the recipe. You want them to feel that they are doing it themselves but within the safety of your guidance.

Chances are, though, even if they're 12 years old, you're not going to give them the recipe book and then leave them alone at home to bake for the very first time. They are children and they need your help to bake a *safe* pie, let alone a perfect one.

Practising music is less dangerous but no less complex. In order to practise consistently and effectively, your child will need to organise their schedule to find a time for practice every day, read the teacher's instructions, and follow the directions while knowing when to change course, as issues arise. Most kids cannot do that. Even most teens will need some help with the scheduling part.

Leave it up to your kiddo and there will probably be no practice pie at all. If you're very lucky, there might be some cereal smushed into a pie dish with whipped cream on top. Yum.

MUSIC IS FUN

So now we're left with the question we started with: Why bake a practice pie at all? You probably wanted your child to start music lessons because:

a) It's a fun hobby.
b) They asked for lessons.
c) You value music education.
d) It will help them develop grit.

Maybe it's a mix of all of those. They are all valid and all excellent reasons to learn music. But really, the first one is the most important. If you make it fun, they will learn more and develop determination and grit over time, as well as reap all the other wonderful benefits of learning music. Fun is the magic ingredient.

To maximise the fun, they need to practise.

This may be a surprise to you. Parents and kids having arguments and groaning matches about music practice is practically a trope at this stage. You might think that if your child has fun in music lessons first, the practice will stem from that. But practice is actually how you have more fun in music.

Let's set our pie ingredients aside for a moment and visit the language department. Imagine you wanted to learn Italian. You love the language and you've heard it's one of the easiest to start with, so you sign up for lessons at your local community centre on Monday evenings. The first week goes great. You learn some simple vocabulary about ordering a coffee and practise it together in the class.

The next Monday you come to your lesson expecting to have just as much fun, but after some pleasantries the teacher launches into a café role play and you're flummoxed. You can't remember a single word from last time and you just stare back at her blankly. She repeats her question three times...but you have no idea what she's saying or how to reply. She's clearly a bit surprised you don't remember anything from last week, but she's kind about it and spends the rest of the lesson reviewing the vocabulary from last week.

Now imagine the same thing happens the following week, and the week after that. It feels as if your mind has been erased of all Italian in the six days between classes. How long would you stick with these lessons if you weren't getting anywhere?

I'm not trying to say that a music student who doesn't practise won't make any progress at all or that a teacher will make them feel bad if they don't. But it's a lot more fun when you feel like you're getting somewhere. It's that forward momentum that will eventually cause your child to become self-motivated to practise and work hard at music even when it's difficult.

So the equation is not:

> *If my child enjoys music,*
> *then they will practise.*

It's:

> *If my child practises,*
> *they're more likely to enjoy music.*

I know that might take some mental adjustment so take a little time to let it sit.

When you're ready, let's get started on that pie so your child can enjoy delicious musical goodness for years to come.

Chapter One

The Pie Dish

Your Practice Habit

A beautiful practice pie dish is where it all begins and where you'll return whenever a pie mishap occurs. You can create the most perfect pie crust and pour in the most sublime filling, but if you then pick it up with your hands and plop it on the oven rack... you're going to have no pie and a very messy oven. You simply cannot do without the dish.

When it comes to music practice, the vessel that holds it all together is the practice routine. If practice isn't happening regularly, no amount of creative and effective practice strategies are going to work. Your goal is to make practice "just something we do", much like brushing our teeth or going to school. Developing a new habit like this is not easy, but it is worth it.

POURING THE MOULD

If we're going to create a solid pie dish, we need to design a dish that fits with our life. There are two basic designs that work for most families: the piggy-back dish and the cuckoo dish.

The piggyback dish works best for many families. To create this pie pan, you'll need to pick something that happens in your family's or child's routine every single day and hitch your little practice piggy dish onto the back of that. For example, if your kiddo always comes home and has a fruit snack after school, practice can come straight after that snack. Or if your child is an early riser, practice could be straight after brushing their teeth while the rest of the family has breakfast.

There are two basic elements you need to make the piggyback dish work. You need something that happens reliably and automatically every day, something that is already a habit. And you need to have a bit of time available after that activity so that practice is not competing with other things. If your child normally has a snack after school and then gets to play video games, inserting practice in between those will not be a popular option.

The cuckoo dish is much simpler but its effectiveness depends on how busy your family's schedule is. To build a cuckoo dish, you need to find a specific time when you're always home and available to practise.

Imagine a cuckoo clock going off at 3:45 pm every day that signals the start of practice time. You could even set an alarm with a cuckoo sound on your phone and make it an inside joke with you and your kiddo.

Again, you need to be careful that this won't be competing with something unfairly. If you let them start watching their favourite show at 3:30 pm, they will not want to go practise at 3:45 pm. That isn't because they don't like music. It's just human nature to be drawn to the easy instant gratification of TV or computer games.

You may find yourselves trying out lots of different pie dish shapes and types in the first several months of lessons, and that's totally normal. Get your child involved in the brainstorming process and treat it as a little science experiment you're running together. You can even keep a scientific log of the results in a lab notebook if you think that would appeal to your child. Here's an example of how that might look:

Date	Title	Results
Sept 1st – 14th	*4:10 Cuckoo clock*	*50% success rate. Was difficult to finish homework in time and when the homework was hard we were too tired for practice.*
Sept 15th – 28th	*Post-catch pre-dinner*	*This was great when it was sunny but we need another plan for when it's raining as no catch happens on those days.*
Sept 29th – Oct 6th	*Breakfast warmup*	*This was hard to remember but worked great when we did it as piano was a welcome distraction while the morning oats were cooking!*

I'm not suggesting you need to run actual experiments on your child, by the way! But many kids will love getting involved in this way and will invest themselves in finding a solution with you.

DECORATING THE PIE DISH

The best pie dishes, like the best pies, are not just functional. They're also beautiful objects that call out to us to use them to create wonderful things. We need to buff, shine and decorate our practice pie dishes by refining the environment in which the child practises.

This is easier with some instruments than others. If your child is learning a portable instrument, I suggest you set up the perfect goldilocks practice spot in your house. It needs to be quiet, calm and comfortable. For many kids, it will also be important that it's not too isolated from the rest of the house. You don't want them to feel as if they're being banished to their room while the rest of the family watches a movie together.

If your child is learning piano, drums or another large stationary instrument and it needs to be in the living room, you'll need to plan for the TV, as it can become a bone of contention for many families, especially in smaller living spaces and open-plan areas. Often, the student is dissuaded from practising because their sibling wants to watch something or play a video game at the same time. Or sometimes the sibling is perfectly quiet and content, but the student can see them playing on an iPad in the corner of their eye and it brings out the green-eyed monster.

Give other family members a heads-up about the routine plan and offer alternative activities for them to do during that time, if necessary, so as to avoid interruptions. The more solid your routine is, the better, as it's easier for the sibling to accept that the student gets the living room at 4 pm on weekdays if they always do and it's reliable, not sporadic and variable.

UNSTICKING A STUCK DISH

From time to time, your pie dish will get wedged in the back of the cupboard. You'll try and try but the confounding thing will just not get out of there! Perhaps the family schedule changed and the old routine just isn't working. Or maybe your kiddo is going through a boundary testing period where they just say no to literally everything you ask them to do, even if it's going out for ice cream.

This is where you might reach for the stickers, reward charts or candy jars. Ideally, we wouldn't need these strategies at all...but that's not reality for many families. Learning to play an instrument is a big and unfathomably long commitment for many children. It takes 10 years or more to become truly proficient, and that kind of dedication may need a nudge or two before they develop their intrinsic motivation to practise based on the reward of seeing results from past practice sessions.

To me, the choice of chart or sticker system you use to get that pesky dish back out of the cupboard when it gets stuck doesn't really matter. But the frame you put it in does.

Do not incentivise the practice; reward the routine.

I don't care if they're working to put the sticker on the chart or saving up monopoly money to buy a hoverboard. Put the emphasis throughout this tracking on the routine, not the practice. Instead of saying, "You need to do your practice every day this week if you're going to go to Leisure Land on Saturday!" tell them that when they hear the cuckoo clock, they must go straight to the piano without you saying anything and that you'll put a tick on the fridge chart when they do.

This might seem pedantic and pernickety of me, but the frame matters. It's important that they don't end up seeing practice as a chore to get through in order to earn a reward, but rather as something they need help *remembering* to do.

START WITH A SINGLE-SERVE PAN

The best thing you can do to maximise your chance of success when you're forging a new pie dish is start small. Your goal should be durability, not size.

A little 10 cm (4 in) pan that is made of cast iron is far superior to a family-sized dish made of sugar lace. The spindly sugar creation might look beautiful, but it's not even going to hold together long enough to bake one pie in it, let alone years of delicious pies in all sorts of flavours.

Start small, stay consistent.

Now, you may have heard the standard advice to practise 30 minutes a day, five days a week. If your teacher told you this personally, I'm definitely not here to argue for you to go against their advice. Every teacher has a different way of doing things that they know works for them in their community.

But, if your teacher has not suggested this to you and you've just heard it on the grapevine, I encourage you to take a different route. I have found that building a routine first is the most crucial thing you can do. Just get your child to their instrument at the same time or same part of the routine every day and follow your teacher's instructions for what to practise. If that lasts no more than five minutes in the beginning, so be it.

You can expand the time your child practises for later, if necessary. In many cases, you won't even need to do this deliberately. Their practice pie dish will naturally expand to fit their assignments and projects inside.

Start with a single-serve pan when your child first begins lessons and any time you fall off the practice bandwagon (and you will, you're human!) and need to cultivate the habit once again.

Chapter Two
Flour

Time Spent

It doesn't matter to me whether you're an almond-flour gal or a spelt stallion or a classic pastry-flour family. All flours are welcome here – as long as they're good quality.

Our goal is that the time your child spends at their instrument really counts. They must be fully present and engaged.

YOUR FAVOURITE FLOUR CONTAINER

I don't know about you, but I've always been a little jealous of *those* people. You know the ones. You peek in their pantry or kitchen cupboard and you see all these beautifully matching containers with elegant hand-drawn lettering on the front declaring what's inside each perfectly stocked vessel.

That's not me. My baking ingredients are all in the paper bags they came in or random mismatched jars and old butter tubs. When I need something I don't use that often I spend 10 minutes removing miscellaneous objects from the back of the cupboard and inspecting them until I find the right one. Then I put all of them back in a different but equally useless and random order.

Whether you're in my camp or the former superhuman one, I want you to resolve to be better with the practice flour.

Every week, your child's teacher entrusts you with this precious musical flour, and you need to go home and put it in a trusty flour container to get it ready for the week of practice ahead. There are three simple things you need to do to pour this practice goodness into its container and secure the lid:

1. Have a conversation with your kiddo about what they did at the lesson.
2. Review the assignments or practice notes the teacher gave you for the week and have your child explain them to you.
3. Trim your child's nails.

That last one may seem out of place, so let me explain. I wrote this book for parents of students of any instrument, but I myself am a piano teacher. And nails that are too long clickety clacking on the keys are not only a pet peeve common to every piano teacher I've met – they also get in the way of developing good technique. The degree to which long nails will get in your child's way will vary, but it is a common issue on many instruments. So ask your teacher what's recommended and then get in the habit of doing this every week as a post-lesson ritual if necessary.

SIFTING THE FLOUR

Your child is not always going to be in an ideal practising mood, day in, day out. Sometimes they'll be tired, distracted, or just a bit off and things won't go as planned. You can definitely maximise the number of productive practice sessions you get, though, by taking a moment to sift the flour with a practice warmup routine.

Different things will be helpful for different children, but a simple place to start is taking three deep breaths together followed by a couple of stretches for the wrists and fingers (your teacher may be able to suggest some appropriate ones).

Creating a habit like this is greater than the sum of its parts. The breathing can help us feel calm and the stretching prepares us to play our instrument. But over time, this pattern of movements will take on a new meaning. Your child's body will learn that this signals the start of practice time and it will become a cue for getting in the right mental mode, too.

FLOURS THAT STICK TOGETHER

You may have noticed above that I didn't say to get your child to take three deep breaths. I said to do it together. Practice will not be a solo activity for the first several years of their lessons. Instead of seeing this as a chore, I'd like to encourage you to treat it as quality time you get to spend with your child. I've heard from many parents that this is one of their favourite times to spend with their child each day as there are no other distractions and they're both completely involved in one activity together.

In this and in everything, each child is unique. Some will love having your support throughout the practice session with you reading each instruction from the teacher and giving suggestions as they repeat tricky passages. Other kids will prefer you sitting nearby reading a book so they know you're there if they need you but don't feel too crowded. Even if your child doesn't want you in the room at all, try to get involved in simple ways such as ducking in to say how much you enjoyed the sound of the hard work that's happening, or asking them for their favourite bit and biggest challenge of the day when they're done.

You do not need to play the instrument or understand music notation to be a helpful practice coach at home. Asking questions about what the teacher advised or getting them to teach you what they learnt at their lesson is all great for reinforcing what the teacher is doing in the lesson.

EXPERIMENTAL FLOUR

Doesn't sound very appealing, does it? I don't think I would buy a bag of flour with that label on the front of it!

But in music and in baking, we need some novelty to keep things interesting. So while your primary aim may be to ensure each practice session is full of quality time and focus, please allow for some play time, too. If your child has already done some good work on their assignments that day, no teacher would begrudge them a few moments to mess around on their instrument and play random note clusters or play old pieces at warp speed or try to figure out the theme to their favourite show by ear. This all helps build their general musicianship – even if sometimes it doesn't look like anything "productive" is happening.

Chapter Three

Water

Listening Habit

You can't make a pie from flour alone. We need some liquid at the very least to make that flour form a dough. If quality time is the flour that provides substance for your crust, water is the inspiration that makes music stick for your child.

You can't be inspired to create a pie if you've never seen or tasted one. And you can't keep the music motivation alive if you don't listen to music and watch others perform it.

HARD WATER AND SOFT WATER

All students need to be surrounded by a broad range of music genres. Depending on your natural inclination, this may be something you need to work hard at or something that happens easily. If you're not in the habit of putting on music in the background, your household currently has "hard water", and if you are, it has "soft water".

For the soft water families that regularly have the radio or playlists on at home or in the car, you simply need to make a little conscious effort to vary the music. I'm not saying you need to put on opera 24/7. You don't even have to listen to opera at all.

Just try to mix it up. Listen to a few different genres you like, whether that's pop, rock, classical, jazz, funk, punk or any other type of music you enjoy.

For me, there is no good music and bad music (though there are definitely child-appropriate lyrics and inappropriate ones); there is just music. A broad listening palette will help your child develop an appreciation for all music has to offer as well as a wider musical vocabulary to draw from in their playing.

Hard water needs some extra help to get going. And so this is where I'm going to ask you to build another new habit. I know you're still working hard on the main practice habit but this one will pay off big time too and should be easier to cultivate. Just pick something you do every day, like driving to school, cooking dinner or folding clothes, that your kiddo is normally present for. Then set an alarm on your phone to remind you to turn on some music at that time. Pick a different playlist each day and experiment as a family with what genres work best.

You can build it into other activities over time but if you're not naturally a big music listener, you don't want to force it. Take it slow and small and then expand if you want to.

FUTURE WATER

I would be surprised if that's not a celebrity-endorsed brand name for bottled water somewhere in the world, but I'm not about to promote a specific product. Big water did not sponsor this book.

The future water I want you to add to your practice pastry is a sprinkling of the music your child will learn to play in the future. Your teacher may be able to direct you to a playlist or make some suggestions of pieces they're likely to learn, or you could look up popular pedagogical pieces for your child's instrument and make your own playlist. If your kiddo is learning piano, you might like to start with my YouTube playlist at colourfulkeys.ie/yeti

Hearing pieces that they may learn someday does two very important things. First, they have the opportunity to get familiar with and excited about these pieces. Students are always itching to learn pieces like Für Elise and Ode to Joy, and it's not because these tunes are particularly fantastic (no offence, Beethoven); it's because they recognise them. It's just fun to learn to play things you've heard others playing so many times and it makes you feel like you're part of the club. Your child can have this feeling with many more pieces if you get in the habit of playing them in your daily life.

The second benefit I see is that it teaches your child that all music is music. The songs their friends sing in the playground are music, so is their parent's favourite car jam, and so are the pieces that they learn to play. It's all music, and it all deserves listening attention.

ALLOWING FOR ABSORPTION

Whether you have a house with hard water (little environmental music) or soft water (lots of music around), you are most likely not allowing for much absorption time. Most music these days (yes, I said "these days" – fair warning that some 19th century nostalgia is on the way) is background music. Music makes us feel things in films, disguises poor-quality microphones in YouTube videos, and attempts to make us stay in shops longer. Most of the time we are not even hearing it, let alone actively listening to it.

Three things are helpful for your child to absorb music more fully: moving, seeing and talking.

Moving to music (AKA dancing) has so many benefits. It's great exercise, it boosts your mood and it helps develop your child's sense of beat and rhythm. Don't worry if you think you're not a good dancer; just think of it as moving your body to the music. That can mean drawing the lyrics in the air, tapping your fork to the beat or stepping side to side. You don't need any complex choreography or fancy moves.

So much of what makes a brilliant performance is not captured in the waveforms of an MP3 file. If it's at all accessible to you, try to take your child to see some live performances. Even if it's just once a year, these occasions will stick with them, and the reasonable prices of tickets at your local music venue, especially for the kid-friendly events they do during the daytime, might surprise you. If there's no way you're making it to a concert hall, then make a habit of watching performance videos together regularly.

Which brings us to the last special absorption aid: talking. When you go to concerts together, watch performances, or listen to new pieces of music – talk about it. Discuss what your kid likes or doesn't like about it. Name the instruments you think you heard (you don't even need to be right!) and ask if they can hear any others. Get your child to describe scenes or stories that could go along with the pieces. Even with music you listen to all the time, there are always new things to discover and discuss, if you really listen.

Chapter Four
Butter

Pride and Mindset

The bulk of your practice pie crust is about quality time. We've made that time stickier by adding active listening, but things are still looking a bit...bland. What's a pie base without at least a little oil or butter? If we use the dough as it is, it's going to be mighty hard to chew through.

Music practice should be enjoyable for your child a lot of the time, but it's also hard work. We need something to make all this dedicated time go a little more smoothly, and the fat that's going to make our pie crust flaky and moreish rather than dry and tough is encouragement from you. Bringing a few carefully chosen comments to the party can make all the difference.

SOFTEN THE BUTTER

Even if your child is at an age when they'll push you away in embarrassment or roll their eyes when you congratulate them, praise from a parent is still one of the most powerful motivators to them. Take it from someone who sees this all the time from the outside: you are their world and the things you say stick.

Which is why you're going to need to be very careful with the kind of praise you offer.

My favourite way to soften the oil or butter for a practice pie crust that consistently yields delicious results is effort-based praise. When you praise a child's effort, you're teaching them to value the work they put in. And that's a large part of what us musicians are usefully addicted to. Many of us enjoy performing, sure, but many more of us get our satisfaction from the practice process. In the beginning, the results from the effort are the reward, but as time goes on, the effort itself becomes satisfying because it is so closely related to the results. Eventually the two are intertwined to the point where the hard work is fun.

Think about anything you do in your own life that's effortful. Whether it's a hobby or your profession, not all of the time you put into it would have been fun to you in the beginning. Learning a complicated new embroidery stitch takes some deciphering and unpicking at the start, but you stick at it because you've seen the fruits of learning complicated stitches before. Once you become a master embroiderer, it's actually fun to discover the challenge of a new stitch you've never seen before. So the best praise you can give your child is effort-based because that will speed up this process. When you focus their attention on the work they put in to make progress, you will train them to value this the most.

Here are some examples of comments that throw light on your child's practice paying off:

- "Wow! Last week you couldn't play through that phrase without stopping. That practice strategy you used made a big difference!"
- "Do you remember last year when doing bouncy notes in one hand and smooth in the other was really challenging? All that practice has made it look easy now because of the hard work you put in."
- "You should be so proud of finishing your book. You stuck with it even though some pieces were challenging and now we're ready for some new musical adventures!"
- "You really focussed during practice this week, and your improvement shows it. You worked on the rhythm, notes and intervals separately before putting it all together. That really worked!"
- "I like the way you tried all kinds of strategies on that section until you got it."
- "It was a big project piece, but you stuck to it and got it done. You worked at it each day, kept up your concentration, and kept following the teacher's instructions. That's great!"

There are many ways to do this, of course, and you'll need to find ways of wording things that feel natural over time. Don't expect instant perfection from yourself, either. Phrases like "Good job!" or "You're so talented!" are not my favourite as they're unspecific and promote a fixed rather than a growth mindset. However, they are so ingrained that they will probably slip out before you even know you're talking. When they do, don't fret. Just follow it up with an effort-based alternative as soon as you can think of one.

MIX IT IN

That lovely praise will keep the butter nice and toasty at room temperature, but if our practice pie is going to get ready for rolling out, we'll need to get out the wooden spoon. Mixing it all together with some statements of fact is the surest way to draw your child's focus in the right direction.

Stating facts might seem dry and unloving, but if you do it with enthusiasm and genuine feeling, these can be some of the most valuable comments for your child.

- "You did it!"
- "You got that right three times in a row!"
- "You did that technique just like your teacher showed us at the lesson!"
- "You remembered the F sharp!"
- "You read the full assignment instructions before starting!"

We don't need to put a judgment (e.g. "that's great" or "you're amazing") on the end of these sentences to make them count. Simply stating the fact of what happened or what is happening lets your child know that you're paying attention and that it matters.

WATCH IT GLISTEN

Sometimes we need to sit back and watch that beautiful pie crust shine in the limelight. To just enjoy the moment and embrace the hard work that went into its creation.

Don't forget to do that with your child's music.

It's easy to show up at a basketball match and scream your support or to proudly display each painting your child brings home from art class on the family noticeboard. With music, however, you need to go a little out of your way to find those glistening moments. Your teacher may host recitals once or twice a year but in between those you can come up with your own opportunities to shine a light on your child's progress:

- Mini-recitals at home: Have your child write a program with their current favourite pieces and organise a set time when everyone will gather on the couch to listen.
- Family singalongs: Once your child gets to a certain level they might be able to accompany a singalong of family favourites.
- School assemblies: Many teachers will be delighted to have a student perform at assemblies or class events if you let them know your child is learning an instrument.

- Phone a friend: Organise a video chat with a friend or family member who doesn't live nearby so that your child can share their newest piece with them.

Not everything needs to be a big production or formal performance. These small opportunities to play for others will increase your child's confidence and give others (besides you) an opportunity to cheer on their progress.

LET IT SIT

Adding the butter or oil isn't all about making things slick or easy. Sometimes, the comment your child really needs is one that acknowledges the reality of the situation.

I've said it before and I'll say it again: learning an instrument is hard. The fact that you need to stick with it and keep working for a long period of time is one of the things that makes it so valuable…but it's also tough. You may be tempted to sweep this struggle under the rug and tell your child to calm down when they're frustrated with the process, and I understand the instinct to want to make everything better as soon as possible. But you need to resist.

Don't say things are easy when they're hard. Don't promise it will be quick when it won't.

Imagine you were complaining to a friend about an annoying coworker who wasn't pulling their weight.

You explain, exasperated, that Jonathan is driving you around the bend and that you have to redo all the work he does which keeps you there an hour after your shift ends each day.

What do you want your friend to say?

Do you want to hear that your problem is easy to fix, if you just talk to him? Do you want to hear that an hour isn't so bad because they frequently have to stay 90 minutes after their shift ends?

No. You want them to say with feeling, "Ugh! Jonathan sounds so irritating!"

You want empathy more than you want a solution, and your child is no different. You can provide strategies and explanations until you're indigo in the ears (the stage after being blue in the face, as I'm sure every parent knows) but you're unlikely to get anywhere with a frustrated child if you don't first acknowledge their feelings. Simple statements like, "Yes, this is hard" and "I can see this is getting frustrating for you", make a big difference in my teaching and I know they can in the practice room, too.

Every time you want to offer a solution or pull your child over a hurdle, stop and ask yourself how your child is feeling and then acknowledge the current reality before you move on to the next step together.

Chapter Five
Salt

Goal Setting

Have you ever forgotten the salt in a recipe? It's easy to skip as it's usually only a tiny fraction of the quantity of the ingredients, but without it the dish will fall completely flat. And if your hand slips and you add a pinch more than intended, it can make your creation positively inedible.

In music practice, it's the goals that we need to treat with this kind of care. Going into a practice session without any idea of what you're trying to achieve or where you're trying to go leads to a lacklustre pie that will likely be thrown in the bin. But create goals that are too grandiose or too detailed and you risk over-seasoning your practice pie to the point of it being off-putting.

MEASURING THE SALT

So what is the right-sized goal for a music student? And what kind of goals should your child set for themselves? For students at all levels, it's best to use the KISS principle here and keep it simple, silly!

Music practice goals do not need to be elaborate or follow a goal-setting framework. They just need to be specific. Some examples of good goals at the beginner level are:

- Play my piece without stopping.
- Count aloud the whole way through.
- Play with the backing track.
- Sing the lyrics as I play.

Once your child is further along, their goals might get more specific, but they shouldn't get more complicated.

- Play section 4 from memory.
- Follow every dynamic marking.
- Play with the metronome at half the performance tempo.
- Sing the bass line while I play the melody.

You can ask your child's teacher for ideas for goals for a specific assignment if you get stuck. But the most important thing about goals in a student's practice, especially for beginners, is their presence. Simply getting your child to state what they're trying to do at the start of the week or the start of a practice session will greatly improve their focus and the sense of achievement when they accomplish that goal. When you know where you're going, you know when you get there.

Chapter Six
Heat

Repetition, Repetition, Repetition.

It's time to put this pie crust in the oven and get it crispy. This requires patience, which can be hard when you want delicious pie *right now*. Take it from someone who knows from experience: you can't just increase the heat to bake it faster. That's called burnt pie and it's what happens to all music students at some stage.

CHOOSING THE RIGHT TEMPERATURE

Every student, young and old, wants to rush to the finished product. It's human nature to want to take a shortcut to the finish line and play the piece, exercise or etude at full tempo ASAP.

The thing is, it's not possible to play a piece just like the recording when you've just started working on it. (If it were, you wouldn't need to work on it.) And turning up the heat (AKA increasing the speed) too soon just leads to a mess that we have to clear up before starting from scratch. It's like running in the wrong direction: you end up farther away from your destination. Practice pies bake best with slow repetitions and lots of them.

FAN OVENS ARE THE FUTURE

Repeating sections or elements of a piece is not most kiddos' idea of a good time. I get how hard it is to go over and over something.

But this is what it takes.

The most effective repetitions are actually those that circulate around like a fan oven.

1. You practise section A a few times.
2. You practise section B a few times.
3. You practise section A a few more times.
4. You practise section C a few times.
5. You practise section B a few more times.
6. You practise section C a few more times.

I think you get the general idea. It's not about the specific pattern I've chosen here; it's about looping back rather than doing 20 repetitions in a row of just one part. This is by far the most efficient form of practice, even if it doesn't feel like it, because it makes your brain work extra hard the whole time.

However, just because a fan oven is the most efficient doesn't mean your child is ready for one yet. Doing interleaved practice like this is hard work and will be off-putting for most beginner students. Most need to work with a conventional oven:

1. Section A 10 times.
2. Piece B 5 times.
3. Exercise C 7 times.

for quite a while before they're ready for the spaced repetition (fan oven) approach. Conventional ovens get the job done just fine so don't force the issue before they're ready. Just have this circular practice idea in your back pocket for when the time feels right.

Chapter Seven
Pie Fillings

Making Practice Fun and Effective

No matter how delicious a pie crust is, no matter how perfectly balanced and crispy, it ain't much without a filling.

The good news is, you've done the hard part. The filling is where we get to have fun and build on that wonderful base to create a practice pie masterpiece.

Unlike the crust, pie fillings can be swapped out for different occasions, invented and reinvented. We're going to start with six basic practice games to begin your child's practice recipe collection. Once they're used to these, the sky's the limit on how many games and strategies you can come up with together!

APPLE

We'll start with apple practice pie because it's a classic, and because the apple has become an international symbol for teacher so it fits right in here.

A good apple practice pie is all about layers. If your pie doesn't have enough layers, it will be an apple tart – refined, elegant and not without charm, but not that hearty practice pie that we're after.

The apple practice pie technique works best with a metronome or drumming app. If you prefer not to use a metronome, feel free to do it without, but your speeds will be more estimated.

Find a speed at which your child can comfortably play through the piece or section without mistakes or pauses, e.g. 60 bpm.

1. Increase 5 bpm and play again.
2. Go back to the comfortable tempo and repeat.
3. Increase 10 bpm and play again.
4. Go back to the comfortable tempo and repeat.
5. Increase 15 bpm and play again.
6. Go back to the comfortable tempo and repeat.
7. Increase 20 bpm and play again.

A good apple practice pie would be made up of 2–4 of these sessions interleaved throughout the practice session. Start with one, though, and work up from there.

CHERRIES

We could just throw all the cherries in a pot and stew them before pouring them into the base…but this cherry pie is for a special occasion. So we're going to lay the cherries out carefully in concentric circles.

1. Choose the most challenging part of your piece. It should be very short, a few notes or perhaps even one chord. This is your most beautiful cherry. Place it carefully in the centre of the pie by playing it very slowly.
2. Now add the note before and after the challenging part and play the slightly longer section, again with great care. This is the next circle of cherries.
3. Continue adding one note at a time to the start and end of the section until you're satisfied that you have enough cherry circles for your pie. I suggest at least tripling the length of the section before moving on.

As you can see, this strategy gets students to play the trickiest part of their piece the most. It also helps them to embed it into the context, which makes it more likely they'll play it successfully when performing the full piece.

PUMPKIN

Pumpkin practice pie is the perfect filling for when your child is getting used to the rhythm and/or fingering patterns in a new piece. They can also use it for any specific passages that are challenging their coordination.

1. Big pumpkin: Drum the rhythm by tapping on your legs. If there are two hands to coordinate (e.g. most piano pieces), each hand should tap its own line.

2. Pumpkin seeds: Tap the pattern with your fingertips on a hard surface like a table or closed piano lid. If your child is learning an instrument where they do not tap downwards (e.g. a string instrument), they can mime playing in the air instead.
3. Smooth pie filling: Play on your instrument.

Your child can repeat this sequence many times in one session to get more comfortable with the patterns.

CHOCOLATE

If you're from North America, you're going to have to bear with me for a second here. You may be familiar with the word "measure" to refer to the sort of boxes we have in music notation. Well, over here we call those "bars" which is why this counts as a chocolate pie.

1. Start at the end of the piece or section and play the last bar (measure).
2. Once you can do this well, play the last two bars (measures).
3. Continue adding on chocolate bars until you reach the beginning of the piece or section. The more chocolate, the better!

Chocolate practice pie is the perfect dish to bring to a party when you don't know much about the tastes of the partygoers. It's a safe bet that chocolate will please most in a crowd, and this is a solid strategy for any piece when you're not sure what needs to be worked on.

BANOFFEE

This is a tried and tested game in my studio that I normally call "crossing the river" but I'm renaming it "banoffee" in honour of this book and my favourite pie. (Yes, I know, controversial! Many people seem to loathe banoffee but I think it's delicious!)

1. Choose a small section of a piece and a simple but specific goal, e.g. play the third line without stopping.
2. Pick three small objects and place them on the left side of your piano or music stand. One is the banana, one is the toffee and one is the cream.
3. Play the section. If you achieve your goal, move the "banana" to the right side of the piano or music stand.
4. Play the section again. If you achieve your goal, move the "toffee" to the right side of the piano or music stand. If you do not, put the "banana" back on the left side.
5. Continue until all three objects are on the right.

This game helps make the idea of playing a section correctly three times in a row into an interactive and rewarding experience. If you ever find your child struggling and getting frustrated by their banoffee, it's likely that their goal is too ambitious. Make the section smaller or the goal easier, and try again.

PECAN

Pecans are, well, a bit nutty really. This is a really fun game to play when you need to bring the giggles into the practice room – stat!

1. Act out the shape of your piece while singing or humming the melody. When it goes up, stretch towards the sky; if it's loud, make a lion face, etc.
2. Figure out the most common note in your piece. Choose a word to replace it and play your piece, but every time you're supposed to play that note, say the word instead.
3. Choose a character from a TV show, book or film. Play your piece in the style of that character, e.g. if you picked a porcupine cartoon maybe it's all staccato and jumpy, or if you chose an easily scared kiddo maybe it's very soft and calm.

These types of activities might seem like pure silliness, but they can actually help your child understand their music in a new way. Pecan shouldn't be the only practice pie your child eats, but it's fine in moderation.

Chapter Eight
Yucky Pie

Troubleshooting Tips

There are many issues and pitfalls that can derail your practice pie baking efforts. These less than desirable results will frustrate you as they come up – you want every pie to be delicious! Try to keep your eye on the bigger prize and know that each and every misstep you or your child makes in the practice pie baking arena can help you improve if you take the time to understand where you strayed from the recipe.

Here we'll briefly run through some of the most common practice mistakes. If your child doesn't make at least a few of these, they're probably not practising enough!

Watch for these issues happening over a prolonged period. An off-week here or there is not a cause for concern; it's just part of the natural ups and downs of the musical journey. Don't worry about taking action until they're happening for a stretch of several weeks.

SOGGY PIE

Yuck, no one wants a soggy pie. This icky and sticky state of a practice pie is usually easy to spot because... your child is simply not practising enough.

If you're generally not at home when practice is supposed to be happening and you think your child may be misremembering the amount of time they practise, this is where having them keep a log or record their sessions may be helpful. But generally, you know when this is the issue. You can see the sogginess of the pie before you even go to cut it.

What to watch for: Less than five days a week of practice, spending less than two hours practising at home each week and slow progress through repertoire.

What to do: Reread the part on page 10 about what to do when your dish gets stuck in the cupboard.

UNDERCOOKED PIE

An undercooked pie happens when your child is putting their practice pie in the oven but not turning on the fan or raising the temperature. They're playing, but they're not doing focussed repetitions.

What to watch for: Pieces seem to sound the same after a whole week of practice, your teacher returns the same comments frequently and practice never sounds messy.

What to do: Try out some of the different pie fillings with your child. They likely need to learn to mix it up a bit before they can learn to practise in a more focussed manner.

BURNT PIE

As I mentioned in the 'Heat' section, burnt pie is one of the most common issues us teachers see. Just like the proverbial hare, students are in a rush to play pieces and end up getting there more slowly because they rush to the finish and trip over themselves in the process.

What to watch for: Smushing notes together or overlapping sounds (depends on the instrument), if there are words, it's too fast to sing along, and you can't tap your foot with their playing because it changes tempo.

What to do: Try out the apple pie filling recipe to work on the skill of repetition and patience in building up the tempo.

DRY PIE

I don't know about you, but I'd take a burnt pie over a dried out and stale one any day. When your child's playing sounds robotic and unenthusiastic, you're probably not spending enough time listening to music together. They need a rich musical environment to draw from to make their playing fun and expressive.

What to watch for: Lack of feeling or dynamics (louds and softs) in your child's playing and declining enthusiasm for their pieces or music in general.

What to do: Review the section about water and add some more music listening into your daily routines.

BLAND PIE

Where dry pie comes from a lack of enthusiasm for music, bland pie stems instead from practice itself feeling boring.

Be careful that you don't mistake issues with practice routine for a bland practice pie. When kids say that they don't want to practise or even that they hate practising, it may be in contrast to the thing they are doing right now. For instance, are you asking them to practise when they've just been playing with a tablet or chatting with a friend? If so, the issue is probably with the way you're building practice into your family timetable rather than with the practice itself.

A bland pie is something quite different. This is about the actual practice activities needing spicing up and/or the need for more goals to provide direction.

What to watch for: Your child groaning during practice sessions even when the assignment is neither too hard nor too easy, or complaining about practice or the instrument being boring when they are not currently practising and a session is not on the immediate horizon.

What to do: Talk to your child about what they want to learn and some fun projects or pieces they have to look forward to soon. Try some of the different practice fillings from the previous section.

OVERWORKING THE DOUGH

I love for parents to be involved in their child's practice. I wouldn't have written this book if I didn't believe that parents need to be empowered to take a greater role in supporting their child's music studies.

But sometimes it does go too far.

And it can be really tough for your child's teacher to tell you this. They don't want to step on any toes and they don't want to talk you out of your enthusiasm for your child's music studies.

So I'm going to lace up my grown-up shoes and do it for them. If you are writing note names (or finger numbers) onto your child's music, correcting all their theory mistakes, or jumping in before they've had a chance to correct their own playing – you are most likely stepping over the line from helpful to hindering.

Now, you absolutely know your child best. Definitely better than me but also better than any other adult in their life, including their music teacher. So if you know they need extra support because they feel insecure or have a specific challenge with music right now, then please, you do you.

I just want you to keep in mind that support can go too far. You can overwork the practice pie dough. This kind of overinvolvement can lead to a young musician whose motivation is entirely external and/ or who cannot work on things independently. Either way, they won't turn into lifelong musicians.

What to watch for: You're writing every note name on your child's music or instrument (e.g. stickers on the piano keys) and your child's teacher did not ask you to, you attend their lessons and answer for them when they don't answer the teacher straight away, and your child has been learning for over a year but you still sit beside them during their practice and make *all* the decisions about what they should do.

What to do: Start to work yourself out of the equation. If your child looks to you for the solution, ask a question instead, or give them an A/B choice. If they check their answer with you, help them walk through checking it themselves. Stay present but make it so they do most of the heavy lifting themselves.

FLAKY CRUST

A practice pie crust that is too flaky is one that breaks apart every time you try to remove it from the dish. If you have built a practice habit more times than you can count, only to lose it after a couple of months or so, your crust is too flaky to be sustainable.

What to watch for: Practice stays consistent for about four weeks but then gradually declines. You feel like every practice habit is built on a foundation of sand and it won't stay up without constant effort from you.

What to do: When the habit is extra hard to build and you've tried different routines and strategies to no avail, don't give up completely! Pick a specific fresh-start date to try again, like the start of a new month or after a special family occasion. Use a practice chart to work on the habit together or keep a practice journal. Treat this as data to help you both find what works, not a tracker that leads to rewards or punishments.

CHEWY CRUST

If your child continues studying a music instrument for more than a year, one thing's for certain: at some point they will be frustrated. This will show up differently for different children, but it will happen. Some will throw a tantrum or break down in tears, some will give up, and others will take it out on you.

These chewy crusts can be hard to digest but (at the risk of sounding old-fashioned or trite) they do build character.

What to watch for: Tears, yelling and other signs of extreme frustration, playing angry and aggressive clusters of random notes (e.g. slapping the piano keys – yes, I have personally done this many times!) and your child saying it's too hard or even "boring" and walking away from their instrument.

What to do: The first step is to acknowledge that what they're feeling is valid. Playing an instrument is difficult and it can be so frustrating when you're trying really hard and can't master a new skill. Always do this with genuine feeling behind your words so that they know you get it.

Next, gauge your child's frustration level. If their emotions are running hot and fast, you'll need to let this chewy pie sit another day to soften up. (I know, this is where our analogy gets a bit gross, but stick with me!) Then, start fresh and walk through the issue that frustrated them in tiny, bite-sized pieces. If it is something beyond your expertise to break down, email their teacher with a heads-up about their frustration with this issue so they can work on some strategies at the next lesson, and simply take it off the practice list for the time being.

Chapter Nine

Bon Appetit!

Enjoy Your Lifelong Pie

I hope by now you feel more confident that you can help your child with their practice, whether or not you can read music, and are starting to see how enriching the practice of practice can be. It's not just a requirement that teachers bundle up into the music lesson. It can also teach your child important life skills and train their brain to be grittier and more resilient.

Baking a practice pie isn't a short-lived sugar high. These are benefits they get to keep for life.

The flipside of that lifelong pie is that each day, each week, each month doesn't matter. Your kiddo is going to have ups and downs on their journey with music. There are going to be times when you run out of flour, the dough won't stick together, or you forget the salt. Do your best to ride these rocky waves when they happen and then start a fresh pie crust when your kid is ready. Learning a music instrument takes a long time, which means you have a lot of margin for error as long as you stay the course and keep going back to the recipe.

I hope you will enjoy every step of your child's pathway through music. Don't rush to some arbitrary destination or definition of success. Sit back with every slice of pie and savour each bite.

Acknowledgements

My first thank-you must go to pie. Thank you for providing me with substantial inspiration for this book and several presentations over the years, and for being such a customisable baking creation. Banoffee is my first love but the full rainbow spectrum of pies have a special place in my heart. Some day I will write an Ode to Pie and sing it to whomever will listen.

Thank you also to my own parents for giving me the opportunity to study music, and to all the parents who have trusted me with their child's music education over the years and who continue to do so. I don't take that trust lightly. I hope this book helps to support many more wonderful parents all over the world as they open up the doors of music for their children.

Finally and most vitally, thank you to my proofreader, Janine Levine. Without her this book would be a muddle of misplaced commas, would have come out several months later than planned, and would have been far less fun to polish to the shiny little gem you're holding in your hands.

More from Nicola Cantan

Thank you for reading *Practice Pie*. If you liked the book, please leave a review wherever you purchased it and tell another music parent who you think would benefit. I'd truly appreciate it.

If you're a music teacher yourself, you may enjoy my other books and resources.

Vibrant Music Teaching

Vibrant Music Teaching is the perfect resource to help you level-up your lessons and teach using more creativity. There is a library of video courses and every printable game and activity you could need for your students. To get more information and sign up for membership, go to: vibrantmusicteaching.com

Thinking Theory Books

Thinking Theory is a series of music theory workbooks designed to accelerate learning while providing plenty of reinforcement of each concept. All concepts are presented in a clear and concise way and no topic is introduced without being revisited several times later in the book. The workbooks incorporate solfa singing, rhythm work and carefully levelled theory concepts. Take a look, at: thinkingtheorybooks.com

Colourful Keys Blog

 I write regular articles and share ideas on my blog, *Colourful Keys*. Check it out if you're looking for more piano teaching inspiration, at: colourfulkeys.com

The Piano Practice Physician's Handbook

 We all know a huge amount of the learning that needs to occur happens in the practice room, not the lesson room. This book (specifically for piano teachers, although many of the ideas can be adapted) will help you to help your students practise more effectively.

Playful Preschool Piano Teaching

 Preschoolers need to move, sing and explore. They need to PLAY. In this book, I've broken down the most effective teaching strategies for preschool piano.

Rhythm in 5

 Many piano students struggle with rhythm, but it's hard to fit in extra rhythm work, and even harder to make it fun. *Rhythm in 5* helps teachers do that with movement and improvisation.

Printed in Great Britain
by Amazon